As Above, So Below

Stars whisper secrets, bright and bold,
Reflections dance on waters cold.
In the night, the truth we find,
Hearts aligned, yet so entwined.

Mountains rise, the valleys sigh,
Echoes travel, reaching high.
Nature's song, a timeless flow,
As it is above, so below.

Sweet Spheres of Emotion

Round the world, emotions spin,
Joy and sorrow, thick and thin.
In each heart, a vibrant hue,
Colors bright, both old and new.

Gentle love, it softly glows,
While the river of longing flows.
In the sky, the sun will rise,
Sweet spheres of love, no disguise.

Celestial Harmony

In the cosmos, notes align,
Each star sings in grand design.
Harmony, a tranquil sound,
In stillness, peace is found.

Galaxies waltz across the night,
Echoing dreams, taking flight.
A cosmic dance, pure and free,
Celestial beings, you and me.

Celestial Handshake

Under the moon, where shadows lie,
Stars converge as moments fly.
Timeless whispers, hands reach wide,
In the dark, no need to hide.

Cosmic ties that intertwine,
Connections made through space and time.
In this dance, we dare to partake,
With every heartbeat, a handshake.

Gravity of Hearts

In the dance of time we twirl,
Holding tight, through the whirl.
Two souls tethered, never apart,
A silent pull, the gravity of hearts.

Stars align in evening's glow,
Whispers soft, like rivers flow.
An orbit traced in love's sweet chart,
Bound forever, the gravity of hearts.

Through storms and trials, we stand tall,
In each other, we won't fall.
A force unseen, yet it imparts,
Endless strength, the gravity of hearts.

Moments pause, the world takes flight,
Cherished dreams ignite the night.
In every beat, a brand new start,
Pulled together, the gravity of hearts.

In gentle sighs, our fears dissolve,
In shared secrets, we evolve.
An infinite dance, an artful part,
Entwined forever, the gravity of hearts.

Radiant Union

In twilight's glow, our spirits blend,
Two paths converge, where dreams ascend.
With every heartbeat, a sacred tune,
In perfect harmony, our radiant union.

The sun dips low, casting its flare,
In your gaze, I find my prayer.
Together we rise, like the noon,
Love's vibrant light, our radiant union.

Through laughter shared and whispers sweet,
In every moment, our souls meet.
A tapestry woven, hearts attune,
In joy we bask, our radiant union.

Seasons change, yet we remain,
Weathering life, through joy and pain.
No distance bold, nor fateful rune,
Can dim the spark of our radiant union.

With hands entwined, we face the night,
Guided by love's eternal light.
A bond unbroken, like the moon,
Forever bright, our radiant union.

Beyond the Nebula

In the vastness where shadows play,
We find our dreams in stardust sway.
Galaxies whisper, old and new,
Together we soar, beyond the nebula.

Time stretches thin in the quiet dark,
Every pulse ignites a spark.
With every breath, new worlds pursue,
Endless journeys, beyond the nebula.

Transcending limits of space and time,
Our spirits dance in cosmic rhyme.
Together we tread, spirits grew,
Uncharted realms, beyond the nebula.

In the rhythmic ebb of cosmic tides,
In silence, love forever glides.
Through astral paths, our spirits flew,
Hand in hand, beyond the nebula.

Stars will fade, but we'll endure,
In love's embrace, we are pure.
Eternally bound, forever true,
Infinite magic, beyond the nebula.

Echoes from the Cosmos

In the silence deep, a call resounds,
Whispers carried on celestial bounds.
Each note a tale of love so true,
Listening close, echoes from the cosmos.

Through the void, a melody flows,
Stars composed in radiant prose.
From light-years past, they bid adieu,
Tales entwined, echoes from the cosmos.

Fragments of dreams, in starlit skies,
Resonate softly, where hope lies.
In distant realms, the heart's view,
Sings a song, echoes from the cosmos.

Moments linger, like dust to air,
In every heartbeat, we share.
The universe hums, painting the blue,
In perfect harmony, echoes from the cosmos.

Together we dance, our spirits rise,
Drifting timeless 'neath endless skies.
With every glance, I see the hue,
Of love's vast depth, echoes from the cosmos.

Celestial Journeys

Stars whisper dreams in the night,
Planets spin with endless delight.
Comets dance across dark skies,
Painting trails of light as they rise.

Nebulas swirl in colors bright,
Guiding travelers through their flight.
Galaxies beckon, far and wide,
In this cosmic realm, we glide.

Light-years pass in a single glance,
In the void, we find our chance.
Wonders await, both vast and grand,
In every corner, a helping hand.

With each star, a story told,
In constellations, old and bold.
Navigating through the unknown,
In the starlit sky, we have grown.

So we journey on, hearts alight,
Through shadows deep and beams of white.
Together in this vast domain,
Celestial paths we shall retain.

Orbital Companionship

Around the sun, we spin in sync,
You and I, we share a link.
Bound by gravity's tender might,
Together we dance through day and night.

In the shadows of the moons we find,
Secrets of the universe, intertwined.
Your warmth, my light, forever near,
In every orbit, I hold you dear.

Through cosmic storms, we bravely steer,
With laughter echoing, conquering fear.
As time unfolds in endless arcs,
Our bond ignites the darkest sparks.

With every rotation, stories unfold,
In the tapestry of the galaxy's gold.
Orbiting each other, we softly sway,
In the silence, love finds its way.

Let the stars witness our gentle flight,
In the realm of space, we shine so bright.
Orbiting together, forever we'll be,
In this endless dance of you and me.

Fables of the Night Sky

Under the blanket of velvet black,
Whispers of myths come flooding back.
Luna leads with her silver gaze,
In the night sky, we lose our haze.

Orion hunts with nimble grace,
While Cassiopeia holds her place.
Each constellation, a tale unfolds,
Of love, courage, and dreams retold.

Shooting stars wish upon the breeze,
In the galaxy's heart, we seek our keys.
Fables etched in starlit dust,
In every twinkle, a sacred trust.

The Milky Way, our guiding lane,
Through the cosmos, we feel no pain.
Endless stories waiting to be spun,
In this universe, we are all one.

So gather 'round, both young and old,
For fables of the night sky told.
In timeless tales, we find our kin,
In every star, our dreams begin.

Hidden Galaxies

Beneath the veil of night's embrace,
Lie hidden galaxies, a secret space.
Whispers of stars that never fade,
In shadows deep, their beauty laid.

Beyond our sight, worlds come alive,
In cosmic realms, where wonders thrive.
Nebulas cradle new suns born,
In their glow, old dreams are worn.

Through telescopes, we search and seek,
For stories of cosmic, ancient peaks.
Mapping the truth behind the stars,
In their light, we heal our scars.

Existence stretches, vast and wide,
Infinity flows like a gentle tide.
In hidden galaxies, fate unfolds,
A treasure trove, a heart of gold.

So let us dream of what lies ahead,
Where the cosmos breathes, and love is fed.
In the universe's arms, we find grace,
Hidden galaxies, our sacred place.

Chasing Shooting Stars

In the velvet sky so bright,
We chase the dreams of night.
Fleeting moments, quick as light,
Wishing on stars, hearts take flight.

Silent whispers in the dark,
Eager souls ignite a spark.
With each glimpse, we leave a mark,
Chasing hopes, our guiding arc.

Through the cosmos, we will roam,
Searching for a place called home.
In the vastness, not alone,
Shooting stars guide us to the unknown.

Every wish, a step we take,
In the name of love, we break.
The night sky holds our fate,
Chasing dreams, we won't forsake.

In the stillness, hearts collide,
Underneath the starry tide.
We chase the glow, nowhere to hide,
In the magic, we abide.

Lightyears of Longing

Distance measured in the dark,
Time slips softly, leaves a mark.
A universe that feels so stark,
Longing echoes, a quiet spark.

In the silence, dreams take flight,
Wishing on the edge of night.
Each heartbeat, a whispered plight,
Lightyears stretch, but love ignites.

Galaxies apart we stand,
Yet forever, hand in hand.
In this vast and lonely land,
Hope's embrace, our futures planned.

Amidst the stars, our hearts entwine,
Counting moments, lost in time.
With every breath, a silent rhyme,
In the distance, love will shine.

Across the void, we find a way,
Through the night, we seek the day.
Lightyears far, yet here we stay,
Longing holds, come what may.

Gravity's Gentle Touch

In the dance of night, we sway,
With gravity, we're drawn to stay.
Softly held in nature's play,
A bond that won't drift away.

Through the whispers of the breeze,
Feel the pull, the gentle tease.
In your arms, I find my ease,
Gravity's love brings me to my knees.

Stars align in silent prayer,
Every moment, love laid bare.
In the push and pull we share,
Together, we become a pair.

Through the orbits, paths unwind,
In this dance, our souls aligned.
Every heartbeat, fate defined,
Gravity binds what fate designed.

As the universe spins around,
In your gaze, I am found.
Underneath the cosmos' sound,
Gravity's touch, forever bound.

Unseen Allegiances

In the shadows where we stand,
Hearts connected, hand in hand.
Secrets kept, a silent band,
Unseen ties across the land.

Through the whispers of the night,
We can feel the hidden light.
Every glance, a spark ignites,
Allegiances beyond our sight.

In the tide of ebb and flow,
Trust the bond, we let it grow.
Through the fog, our feelings show,
Unseen forces guide our flow.

In this maze, we find our way,
Through the chaos, come what may.
Every step, a choice we play,
Together always, night or day.

With each heartbeat, we unite,
Navigating through the night.
In the stillness, pure delight,
Unseen allegiances, our light.

Polishing Stars Together

Under the velvet sky, we stand,
With dreams that shimmer in our hands.
We reach for orbs that twinkle bright,
In the embrace of whispers and light.

Our laughter dances in the air,
As we share the weight of our cares.
Each breath we take, a gentle spark,
Polishing stars in this endless dark.

Wishing upon each gleaming sphere,
Casting away doubt and fear.
Together we mend the cosmic seams,
Woven in the fabric of our dreams.

In the canvas of this night,
Our spirits weave, our hearts take flight.
Through the stillness, our voices call,
A duet that echoes, binding us all.

Stardust flows through our fingers fine,
In this moment, your heart aligns.
We polish stars, our hopes entwined,
Creating worlds, our souls combined.

Starlit Threads

In the tapestry of night so wide,
We trace the paths where spirits glide.
Stars above, like stories, glow,
Unraveling tales that softly flow.

Casting nets of silken dreams,
Catching glimmers, weaving beams.
Each twinkling light a thread we find,
Stitched in time, our hearts aligned.

Whispers echo in the cosmic dance,
As we sway in the starry romance.
Interlaced destinies, bold and bright,
Guiding us through the endless night.

In this celestial loom, we play,
Sending wishes into the fray.
With every heartbeat, a spark ignites,
A path illuminated by heart's delight.

Stepping softly on celestial trails,
Our laughter intertwines, love prevails.
Together, we create a universe vast,
In starlit threads, forever cast.

Interwoven Destinies

In the quiet dawn, our paths align,
Two souls bound by the grand design.
With every glance, a story's told,
In whispered dreams, our hearts unfold.

We dance through galaxies yet unknown,
Within the light, our spirits grown.
Together we venture, hand in hand,
Interwoven destinies, carefully planned.

The universe sings as we embrace,
In every heartbeat, we leave our trace.
Through cosmic winds, we soar so high,
Navigating the vast, starry sky.

In the weave of time, we craft our fate,
Sewing moments, both small and great.
With threads of love, we stitch and tear,
Creating a journey beyond compare.

Every star a promise, every breath a wish,
Bound together in love's sweet bliss.
Destinies intertwine, forever to last,
A cosmic bond, unbreakable and vast.

Charts of the Heart

With maps etched in our souls, we start,
Navigating the charts of the heart.
Every line a story that's yet to unfold,
Guiding us where love is bold.

Through valleys of doubt and peaks of joy,
We traverse together, girl and boy.
Drawn by the compass of dreams so clear,
In each other's arms, we find no fear.

The stars align as we make our way,
In every turn, we softly sway.
Finding treasures in the sands of time,
Building a love so pure, so prime.

With every pulse, new journeys start,
Following the rhythm of the heart.
Through storms and calm, together we steer,
Creating a map we hold so dear.

So let us sail through night and day,
On the seas where passion will play.
With charts of the heart, our spirits soar,
Forever united, we lovingly explore.

Celestial Rhapsody

In the silent night sky,
Stars whisper tales of old.
Constellations dance high,
In silver threads, they unfold.

Comets streak like dreams,
Crossing paths with our hearts.
In this cosmic scheme,
Eternal love never parts.

Galaxies swirl about,
In a vibrant, endless spin.
Their light is a shout,
Of all the love within.

Underneath the pale moon,
Soft shadows weave and drift.
In this tranquil tune,
Hearts find their gentle lift.

Embers of light do play,
In the vastness we explore.
Each night leads the way,
To find what we adore.

Bonds Unwritten

In the quiet of souls,
A connection starts to grow.
Invisible, hidden roles,
We share what we both know.

Eyes that meet in silence,
Speak volumes without sound.
With every small glance,
A deeper bond is found.

Laughter shared in twilight,
Echoes of joy and care.
Each moment feels so right,
A promise in the air.

Fingers brush, a soft spark,
Igniting flames of trust.
Guided by the dark,
Our spirits feel a lust.

Though words may not be spoken,
Our hearts know every thread.
In a tapestry unbroken,
A love that lies ahead.

Tidal Forces of Affection

Waves crash upon the shore,
As hearts begin to blend.
In rhythms we explore,
A love that knows no end.

The moon pulls at our souls,
With secrets wrapped in light.
In its glow, love rolls,
Through the shadows of the night.

Each tide comes in with grace,
Caressing the barren sand.
In this sacred space,
We'll always take a stand.

When storms threaten to rise,
We'll anchor ourselves tight.
Together, past the skies,
We'll find our way to light.

Forever drawn we'll be,
By the pull of heart's design.
In love's vast, endless sea,
Together we will shine.

Radiance of Remembrance

In the flicker of a flame,
Memories softly glow.
Every spark holds a name,
Of moments we both know.

Time weaves a tapestry,
In threads of joy and pain.
Each stitch a memory,
In sunshine and in rain.

Voices whisper through the haze,
Echoes of laughter shared.
In twilight's gentle gaze,
Our bond remains declared.

Photographs fade with age,
Yet feelings stay alive.
In each tender page,
The heart learns to survive.

Through the radiance we find,
What once was lost in time.
Memory, sweet and kind,
Writes our quiet rhyme.

Astral Adoration

In twilight's glow, we gaze afar,
Beneath the watchful, silver star.
Whispers of the cosmos call,
In dreamy realms where starlight falls.

Dancing shadows, ethereal grace,
We wander through this boundless space.
Heartbeats sync with the universe,
In this cosmic love, we immerse.

Celestial bodies weave their fate,
As planets spin, we meditate.
With open hearts, we share a wish,
In astral waves, we find our bliss.

Galaxies twirl like lovers' sighs,
In the silence, passion lies.
Every twinkle, a promise made,
In the void, our love won't fade.

Together we drift on stardust trails,
Through nebulae where beauty prevails.
In the night, we love and learn,
For in the stars, our hearts do burn.

Planetary Pulse

Beneath the sky, our hearts align,
In rhythm, like the stars we shine.
A pulse that travels through the night,
Guided by the moon's soft light.

Orbits dance with a steady grace,
As we find our sacred place.
The planets sing a lullaby,
In harmony, we soar and fly.

Waves of energy collide and surge,
Interstellar love, a vivid urge.
In every heartbeat, we connect,
A force unseen, our hearts reflect.

Tides of cosmos, ebb and flow,
In this journey, we come to know.
The universe, a canvas wide,
Painted with dreams, side by side.

Galactic winds may drift us far,
But you're my steady, guiding star.
Together, we'll embrace the night,
In planetary dance, pure delight.

Dark Matter and Dreams

In shadows deep, where thoughts reside,
Dark matter holds what we can't hide.
Dreams linger softly in the air,
Whispers of hope, a secret prayer.

Through silence thick, our visions flow,
Unknown paths where the starlight glows.
Navigating through the unseen threads,
In cosmic realms where the mystery spreads.

Glimmers of truth in the dark abyss,
A chase for wonders, moments of bliss.
We delve into realms that time has missed,
In the darkness, our dreams exist.

Gravity pulls, yet we remain light,
Our spirits soar in the endless night.
With each heartbeat, we weave a tale,
Of dark matter and dreams we hail.

Awake or asleep, we dance through space,
Finding solace in each embrace.
In the deep void, we aren't alone,
For in our dreams, we've brightly shone.

The Space Between Us

In the vastness where shadows meet,
There's a silence, soft and sweet.
In every pause, a story lies,
In the space, our longing sighs.

Fleeting moments, time stands still,
The air is charged, electric thrill.
A heartbeat echoes, a fleeting touch,
In the stillness, we feel so much.

Where galaxies drift and hopes ignite,
In this emptiness, we find our light.
Every gap filled with whispered dreams,
In the universe, nothing is as it seems.

Through the void, we reach for more,
In the space between, we've begun to soar.
And though we stand in mystery's thrall,
In love's embrace, we conquer all.

With every breath, we share a spark,
In the melody sung in the dark.
Together we bridge the cosmic divide,
For in this space, our hearts collide.

Ether's Embrace

In whispers soft where shadows play,
The stars above begin to sway.
With each breath, the cosmos sighs,
In silent songs, the spirit flies.

Veils of light dance through the air,
Each note a promise, rare and fair.
Embraced by dreams, we drift along,
In the silence, we find our song.

Time unravels, weaving threads,
Of forgotten tales, whispers shed.
In this realm, dreams take their flight,
Bound by the pulse of endless night.

Awake, we soar on wings unseen,
In ether's hold, where we've been.
Every heartbeat, a chance to feel,
The cosmic truth, the wounds we heal.

Together we'll bask in unity's glow,
In the Ether's arms, where love will grow.
Each moment treasured, a gentle trace,
A timeless waltz in Ether's embrace.

The Tapestry of the Night

In the fabric of night, threads intertwine,
Stars like jewels, a shimmering line.
Moonlit whispers wrap the earth,
Cradled softly in silent mirth.

Each scream of the owl, a tale to share,
Of shadowy figures that linger near.
The breeze in the trees sings lullabies,
While dreams take flight, beneath the skies.

Woven stories in twilight's fold,
Every heartbeat, a secret told.
A canvas painted in shades of dark,
Where lost souls find their needed spark.

Night's tender veil, a soft embrace,
Offers comfort, a sacred space.
In starlit corners, hopes ignite,
Revealing wonders of the night.

Together we roam, through starlit trails,
In the tapestry of night, our love prevails.
Bound by dreams, in moon's soft light,
Eternal moments in shared delight.

Galactic Concord

In the vastness, where silence dwells,
Among the stars, the universe tells.
A symphony bright, of cosmic song,
In Galactic Concord, we all belong.

Celestial bodies in graceful dance,
Each twinkle a call, a wondrous chance.
Galaxies twirl in an endless embrace,
Uniting worlds in a sacred space.

Time dissolves, as we drift along,
In harmony, every heart sings strong.
Unseen connections weave us close,
In the depths of the infinite, we chose.

From the depths of space, a message flows,
In the harmony of stars, love grows.
Together we rise, in radiant light,
In Galactic Concord, we find our sight.

In this union of spirits, we soar,
Through cosmic realms, forever more.
Each heartbeat echoes in starry lore,
In Galactic Concord, we are evermore.

Harmony in the Heavens

Stars whisper softly at night,
Moonlight dances, pure and bright.
In the stillness, hearts unite,
Embraced by cosmic flight.

Galaxies swirl, a vast ballet,
Each twinkle holds a secret sway.
Nature's chorus, night and day,
Guides our spirits on their way.

Waves of light through darkness weave,
Infinitesimal dreams conceive.
Together in the night we believe,
In harmony, we find reprieve.

Planets spin in graceful arcs,
Their beauty ignites cosmic sparks.
Through the void, love leaves its marks,
In the canvas of the dark.

Eternal bonds in the stardust flow,
Connected in a celestial glow.
Unified, our souls will grow,
In harmony, forever we know.

Ethereal Ties

In the silence between the stars,
Our spirit sings, no earthly bars.
Ethereal ties stretch beyond,
A journey deep, our souls respond.

Veils of light wrap us in dreams,
Together in this world, or so it seems.
Threads of fate in cosmic streams,
Through the universe, love redeems.

Every heartbeat aligns with time,
A rhythm sweet, a perfect chime.
Celestial dance, so sublime,
In the vastness, our hearts climb.

With every glance, our worlds collide,
In galaxies where love won't hide.
United in this timeless ride,
Ethereal ties forever abide.

As dawn breaks, we float anew,
In endless skies, a deeper hue.
Together always, just me and you,
In the cosmos, love shines through.

Celestial Threads

Woven into the fabric of night,
Celestial threads glimmer, ignite.
In shadows deep where dreams reside,
They bind us close, side by side.

Stars entwined in the velvet sky,
Every twinkle, a tender sigh.
We traverse space, you and I,
Boundless love that can't deny.

Galactic winds whisper our names,
Fueling the heart's eternal flames.
In silence, we play the cosmic games,
As destiny calls, it never blames.

Every heartbeat echoes the past,
In a universe so vast, so vast.
Our connection, steadfast and fast,
Together always, ever last.

As we drift among the spheres,
Woven together through laughter and tears,
Celestial threads, devoid of fears,
In this infinite love, our path clears.

Intergalactic Affection

Crossing over the stars we roam,
Finding love in the great unknown.
Intergalactic affection flows,
In the silence, our spirit glows.

Nebulae cradle our dreams so bright,
A tapestry woven in the night.
In each embrace, the cosmos sighs,
As galaxies spin, our love defies.

Functions of time and space entwine,
In your arms, the universe aligns.
Gravity pulls, our souls combine,
In this vast expanse, you're forever mine.

Across the cosmos, we'll journey far,
Our love a radiant, guiding star.
No boundaries here, just who we are,
In the infinite, we raise the bar.

For in this void, we find our place,
Intergalactic love, a warm embrace.
As we dance among the stars with grace,
In this affection, we find solace.

Voyager of the Heart

In the depths of silence, I roam free,
Seeking whispers, where love might be.
Stars above guide my yearning soul,
In the void, I search to feel whole.

With every breath, I call your name,
Through distant worlds, I seek the flame.
Hearts entwined in a cosmic dance,
Fate has drawn us to this chance.

In realms unknown, our paths align,
Every heartbeat, a gentle sign.
Adrift in dreams, I sail the seas,
Where love's embrace is meant to please.

With each encounter, a story grows,
In tender moments, our essence flows.
Through endless nights, we chart our course,
In love's vast ocean, we find the source.

Together we wander, hand in hand,
Voices in the wind, a sweet demand.
The voyager of the heart shall find,
A love that lingers, forever entwined.

Astral Auras

In the twilight glow, the worlds converge,
Colors of stardust begin to surge.
Auras shimmer, a radiant light,
In this cosmic dance, we take flight.

With every hue, a story unfolds,
A tapestry woven with dreams bold.
In celestial realms, our visions soar,
Guided by sparks, we crave for more.

Whispers of galaxies, soft and sweet,
In astral embrace, our hearts shall meet.
In the silence of space, we explore,
Echoes of love on an infinite shore.

Stars align as we draw near,
In the canvas of night, we hold dear.
Magic ignites in this vibrant haze,
In astral auras, we find our ways.

Lost in the cosmos, we weave our fates,
In the glow of love, the universe waits.
Together we dance, a celestial art,
In the infinite realm of the beating heart.

Navigating the Night

Under a veil of velvet skies,
The night unfolds, and softly sighs.
Moonlit paths guide our feet,
In shadows deep, our hearts shall meet.

With constellations as our guide,
Through mystic lands, we shall abide.
Winds of destiny whisper low,
In twilight's glow, our spirits flow.

Each star a wish, a dream to chase,
In the stillness, we find our space.
Navigating through the darkened veil,
In the night's embrace, we shall not fail.

As dawn approaches, we hold tight,
The memories made in the quiet night.
Through endless journeys, love ignites,
Navigating paths of golden lights.

In the tapestry of dusk and dawn,
With open hearts, we venture on.
Navigating the night with grace,
In love's vast arms, we find our place.

Cosmic Connections

In the silence of space, we intertwine,
Two souls adrift, an endless line.
Cosmic threads weave through the air,
In this vastness, we find what's rare.

With every heartbeat, a pull we feel,
In the universe, our fate is sealed.
Stars above whisper secrets sweet,
In cosmic connections, our hearts meet.

Through galaxies far, we journey wide,
Hand in hand, we face the tide.
A dance of souls across the sky,
With every moment, we learn to fly.

In the embrace of infinity's grace,
We find our rhythm in this space.
Each light a promise, a love that grows,
In cosmic connections, our truth shows.

Together we shine, a radiant beam,
In the depths of night, we dare to dream.
With cosmic hearts, we craft our song,
In this vast universe, we belong.

Starlit Whispers

In the quiet of night, stars gleam,
Whispers of light, a celestial dream.
Softly they dance in the vast above,
Carrying tales of heart and love.

The moon smiles down, casting its glow,
Guiding lost souls through shadows below.
A gentle hush sweeps through the air,
Nature's lullaby, a song rare.

Crickets sing sweet in the cool breeze,
While leaves rustle softly among the trees.
Each twinkle holds a wish untold,
An echo of dreams both brave and bold.

Beneath the sky's vast, sprawling maze,
We find our peace in the starlit haze.
With every blink, a story unfolds,
In the universe's canvas, tales of old.

So let us wander in this night,
Hand in hand under stars so bright.
In starlit whispers, hearts will meet,
Where silence brings a love so sweet.

Threads of the Cosmos

Woven in silence, the cosmos sings,
Threads of existence on delicate wings.
Galaxies swirl in a dance divine,
Connecting our souls, a boundless line.

Nebulae glow in colors so rare,
Mapping the paths of time and air.
Each star a stitch in the fabric wide,
A harmony found where dreams reside.

Across the vastness, our spirits roam,
Seeking the light that calls us home.
In every heartbeat, the universe sways,
Guiding us softly through starry arrays.

In unity forged from cosmic dust,
We hold the secrets, in starlight we trust.
A network of wonders that never ends,
Threads of the cosmos, where love transcends.

As we gaze upwards, let our hearts soar,
Embraced by the twinkle forevermore.
In this grand tapestry, we find our place,
Threads of the cosmos, woven with grace.

Lunar Embrace

Under the moon's tender embrace,
We find solace in its silver grace.
A beacon of hope in the night so deep,
A guardian's watch as the world sleeps.

Shadows play softly on fields of gold,
Secrets of the night quietly told.
With each gentle glow, worries will flee,
Wrapped in the warmth of moonlit glee.

Starlight ignites in the ocean's tide,
Reflecting dreams where our hearts collide.
In the stillness, our spirits ignite,
Guided together through the velvet night.

The moon whispers tales of joy and despair,
A lover's promise carried through air.
In its glow, our fears start to fade,
Embraced by the light that the heavens made.

So let us linger beneath the night's dome,
In lunar embrace, we shall find home.
With each phase of the moon overhead,
Our hearts intertwine in the love we spread.

Constellations of Connection

In the night's canvas, connections gleam,
Constellations form in a shared dream.
Stars align, forging bonds so bright,
A journey together, guided by light.

In every twinkle, a story we share,
Mapping our journeys in the midnight air.
Through trials and triumphs, we find the way,
In constellations, our hearts play.

Celestial paths intertwine and blend,
Each star a reminder of love, our friend.
We are all threads in this cosmic design,
Intertwined destinies, yours and mine.

As we stargaze under the vast sky,
Let the whispers of stars lift us high.
In the silence of night, our hopes take flight,
Guided by constellations, pure and bright.

With every glance at the heavens above,
We feel the warmth of this mighty love.
In constellations of connection, we find,
Eternal bonds of the heart and mind.

Beyond the Infinite

A cosmos wide, a dance of light,
Galaxies swirl, igniting the night.
Dreams of wanderers, bold and free,
Whispers of worlds, calling to me.

Time's embrace, a timeless chase,
In the dark, we find our place.
Echoes of thoughts, like stars they gleam,
In the void, we weave our dream.

Fleeting moments, forever last,
In the silence, we rise from the past.
Hearts intertwined, a cosmic blend,
On this journey, no need to pretend.

Chasing comets, riding the waves,
Through the starlit paths, the fearless braves.
Beyond the edge, we find our space,
In the infinite dance, we find grace.

Beyond the gaze of earthly bounds,
In the celestial, our love resounds.
To eternity, hand in hand,
Beyond the stars, we take our stand.

Love Among the Stars

In the twilight, soft and bright,
Two souls find warmth, in starry night.
Whispers shared, a gentle glow,
In the dark, our spirits flow.

Orbits align, a radiant spark,
In the cosmos, we leave our mark.
Fates entwined, like constellations,
Guiding us with sweet vibrations.

Echoes of laughter, in silver skies,
Every glance, love never lies.
Together we dream, unafraid to soar,
Forever together, we desire more.

In the stillness, our hearts collide,
Among the stars, we dream, abide.
Invisible threads weave through the night,
Drawing us close, in pure delight.

With every twinkle, my heart you seize,
In the universe, we find our peace.
Love's gravity, a timeless force,
Among the stars, we chart our course.

Glimmers of Togetherness

Softly shining, a glimmering spark,
Illuminates the edges of the dark.
In each breath, the warmth we share,
Threads of joy, woven with care.

In quiet moments, echoes will rise,
Reflecting dreams, like fireflies.
Hand in hand, we walk along,
In our hearts, we sing a song.

Through the storm, we'll find our way,
United souls, come what may.
Glimmers bright, in darkest hours,
Blooming love, like springtime flowers.

With each laugh, a shimmer of light,
Together we shine, banishing night.
In the tapestry of fate, we weave,
Glimmers of hope, in love, believe.

Through life's journey, hand in hand,
In every moment, together we stand.
Beyond the struggles, we find our rest,
Glimmers of togetherness, truly blessed.

Connexions in the Void

In the silence, we find the sound,
Connecting threads that wrap around.
In the shadows, our spirits reach,
Intimate bonds, no words can teach.

Floating far, yet close in heart,
In the void, we are a part.
Galaxies collide, forming anew,
In the vast, I am with you.

Through the darkest, the starlight guides,
Within the space, our love abides.
Reach for me, across the night,
In the void, we find our light.

Infinite dreams weave through the air,
In each heartbeat, a silent prayer.
From the depths, our voices rise,
Connexions bloom, beneath the skies.

Together we navigate the unknown,
In the emptiness, we are not alone.
In the stillness, our hearts ignite,
Connexions in the void, pure and bright.

Starlit Embrace

Under a velvet sky so deep,
Stars awake from their ancient sleep.
Whispers of dreams dance in the air,
In this embrace, we lose all care.

The night wraps us in a gentle hold,
Stories of the universe unfold.
With each twinkle, secrets are shared,
In this moment, we are ensnared.

Galaxies spin in a silent song,
With every heartbeat, we belong.
Together we shine, two souls ignited,
In the darkness, forever united.

As comets streak across the skies,
We trace the paths with longing sighs.
Hand in hand, we wander free,
In starlit realms, just you and me.

With whispered wishes, time stands still,
Eternity beckons with a heart's thrill.
In this embrace, we find our place,
Forever lost in the starlit space.

Tethered by the Moonlight

Moonlight bathes the world in glow,
Tethered hearts, where soft winds blow.
In its light, our spirits soar,
Bound together, forevermore.

Shadows dance upon the ground,
In silence, our love is found.
Each silver beam, a thread so tight,
Filling the dark with pure delight.

We wander paths of glimmering dreams,
Following the night's soft themes.
Hand in hand, as time drifts by,
Under the watchful, watchful sky.

Every whisper of the night wind,
Reminds us how our hearts are pinned.
In moonlight's glow, the world stands still,
An endless journey, an endless thrill.

As stars twinkle with secret glee,
We share our hearts, you and me.
Forever tethered in this light,
Bound together by the night.

Cosmic Whispers

In the quiet of a cosmic night,
Whispers drift, glowing bright.
Galaxies sing their ancient lore,
Echoes of love forevermore.

Stardust falls like softest rain,
Carrying dreams, joy, and pain.
With each breath, the universe sighs,
Painting wonders across the skies.

In this vastness, I find your face,
Every star, a sacred place.
We share secrets, profound and true,
In cosmic whispers, just me and you.

Luminous threads connect our souls,
In the fabric of space, we're whole.
With every flicker, hope ignites,
Guided by the celestial lights.

Through the cosmos, our hearts entwine,
In every glance, a cosmic sign.
With whispered love, we rise above,
Forever bound in the starlit love.

Constellations of Connection

In constellations bright and bold,
Stories of our love unfold.
Each star a promise, shining clear,
Guiding our hearts, always near.

Galaxies spin in timeless dance,
In their rhythm, we find our chance.
With every shimmer, fate aligns,
Two souls merged, a love that binds.

Nebulas form like dreams we craft,
Leading us to our sacred path.
In the cosmos, we trace our fate,
Bound by love, we celebrate.

As night wraps us in its embrace,
We find a home in this vast space.
Every twinkle, a touch so sweet,
In cosmic realms, where lovers meet.

Together we write our story bright,
Through the darkness, we are light.
In constellations, our love's reflection,
Everlasting, pure connection.

Orbiting Solitude

In silence deep, I drift alone,
Stars above, a distant throne.
Each heartbeat counts the passing light,
In the void, I seek the night.

Shadows dance with glimmering dust,
A cosmic realm, in dreams I trust.
Galaxies swirl, a silent scream,
Orbiting in a timeless dream.

Whispers echo through the dark,
In this space, I leave my mark.
Fleeting thoughts, a binary code,
In solitude, I walk this road.

Here I float, both free and bound,
In the stillness, silence found.
While worlds collide and comets race,
I find peace in empty space.

Every star, a tale untold,
In their glow, I'm brave, not cold.
Orbiting quiet, heartbeats slow,
In solitude, I learn to grow.

Whispers of the Wide Universe

In the hush where shadows play,
Stars conspire, night turns day.
Whispers drift on cosmic winds,
Tales of love where dreaming begins.

Galaxies shimmer, stories unfold,
Secrets hidden, yet to be told.
Neon lights of distant spheres,
Fill the void with ancient fears.

Patterns dance in quiet grace,
Light travels far, time leaves no trace.
Whispers sing from distant spheres,
Carrying dreams across the years.

In the twilight's gentle glow,
The universe, a vast tableau.
Each twinkle, a story spun,
Underneath this endless sun.

Marvel at the night so vast,
Future, present, ripples past.
In every echo, every sigh,
Whispers call as time flies by.

Celestial Wishes

Underneath the starlit sky,
I find solace, questions nigh.
For every wish upon a star,
A gentle hope, no dream too far.

As comets blaze their fiery trails,
In their wake, our courage sails.
To grasp the light and hold it tight,
Celestial dreams in endless night.

With every pulse, the cosmos hums,
A symphony of distant drums.
Wishes born in silent prayer,
In the dark, they shimmer fair.

The universe, a canvas wide,
Painting dreams with cosmic tide.
Let each star, a wish ignited,
Guide the lost, the lonely, and excited.

As the night enfolds my heart,
I send my dreams to worlds apart.
With each blink, a wish takes flight,
In the arms of endless night.

Secrets of the Starry Path

On the path where stardust flows,
Whispers of the night wind blows.
Secrets kept in silver glow,
Lead my steps where few dare go.

Each constellation tells a tale,
Of lovers lost and ships that sail.
Inky skies, a map unfurled,
Guiding souls across the world.

Nebulas spill their colored light,
Painting dreams in the velvet night.
Follow echoes left behind,
In secrets shared, the lost we find.

With every twinkle, paths align,
A tapestry of fate divine.
In the cosmos, we are one,
Bathed in light from moon and sun.

Discovering what lies ahead,
On the starry path, we tread.
In every shadow, every beam,
Secrets whisper, guiding dream.

Cosmic Compatriots

In the vastness, we unite,
Stardust whispers in the night.
Planets spin in joyful dance,
Bound together, caught in chance.

Celestial hearts, we gleam and glow,
Through the darkness, warm and slow.
In orbits close, our spirits soar,
Companions bright, forevermore.

Across the tides of time and space,
We share this wondrous, timeless place.
Galaxies laugh, entwined in light,
Cosmic friends, in endless flight.

Through the nebula, hand in hand,
We journey forth, a starry band.
Embers flicker, dreams alight,
Together bold, we face the night.

With every pulse, our love expands,
Infinity wrapped in gentle hands.
In every star, our story we write,
Cosmic compatriots, shining bright.

Aurora of Affection

Beneath the skies of vivid hue,
A dance of lights, for me and you.
Whispers soft in colors play,
Auroras warm both night and day.

In silken waves, together we sing,
Nature's symphony, love takes wing.
Every flicker, a promise new,
In the cosmos, just me and you.

Caught in this magical embrace,
We move as one, in perfect grace.
With every shade, our hearts align,
Under the canvas, love divine.

Through shimmering greens and golden beams,
We cast our hopes, embrace our dreams.
In each bright flash, affection glows,
A tapestry of warmth it shows.

With every dawn, our spirits rise,
Painting love across the skies.
Together shining, pure connection,
Lost in this aurora of affection.

Galactic Footprints

In the dust of stars we roam,
Leaving traces, far from home.
Across the cosmos, hand in hand,
We explore this uncharted land.

Every step a story told,
In glowing trails of cosmic gold.
Together we mark this endless space,
In galactic footprints, find our place.

Time unfolds in spiraled grace,
As we race through this vast place.
Constellations guide our way,
In every night, a brand new day.

With every leap, a new song flows,
In celestial rhythms, love bestows.
As galaxies spin, our paths entwine,
In cosmic dance, your heart in mine.

Through the silence of the night,
We chase the stars, our hearts alight.
In every corner, we leave our mark,
Galactic footprints shine in the dark.

Love Beyond the Veil

In shadows cast, our love does dwell,
A timeless bond, a sacred spell.
Beyond the veil where spirits play,
Forever joined, we find our way.

In whispers soft, the universe sighs,
Two hearts merged in endless skies.
Through darkness deep, we light the night,
With every dream, our hopes take flight.

In the stillness, echoes call,
A love that conquers, conquers all.
Though worlds may part, our souls will weave,
In every heartbeat, we believe.

Through realms unseen, together we rise,
Beneath the moon, a million ties.
With stardust wrapped, we sing our fate,
Love beyond the veil, it's never late.

Together we dance in a timeless flow,
In every shadow, our love will glow.
As stars align and fates entwine,
Beyond the veil, eternally thine.

Starlight Ties

In the hush of night we muse,
Stars cast down their gentle hues.
Whispers travel through the void,
Binding souls, no hearts destroyed.

Across the dark, our wishes fly,
Woven dreams in velvet sky.
Each glimmering light a thread,
Connecting paths where we are led.

Beneath the cosmos' endless gaze,
We dance in fate's tender blaze.
In starlight's glow, we find our way,
Together through the night and day.

All the worlds we could explore,
Holding hands, we seek for more.
In every flicker, hope ignites,
Our bond is forged in starlight ties.

The Universe in Our Hands

In twilight's veil, we stand so near,
The universe, so vast, yet clear.
With fingertips, we brush the stars,
Creating dreams that travel far.

Galaxies spin in endless night,
While we hold tightly to our light.
Each moment shared a precious spark,
Illuminating paths through dark.

Together we can shape and mold,
Stories waiting to be told.
In the vastness, we find our place,
Every heartbeat a warm embrace.

Mirrors reflecting what we feel,
Love and hope, they intertwine and heal.
In our palms, we cradle skies,
The universe in our hands relies.

So let the cosmos whisper low,
A symphony of stars to grow.
In unity, we take a stand,
The infinite, in heart and hand.

Aetherial Interlude

In realms where silence softly dwells,
An aether's tune, the heart compels.
Glimmers of light that dance and weave,
An interlude for those who believe.

Beneath the arch of endless dreams,
The world is painted in moonlit beams.
Moments linger, pure and sweet,
Time halts as our souls repeat.

Echoes whisper, softly soar,
In timeless grace, we yearn for more.
With every breath, the magic flows,
In the warm embrace of night's soft prose.

Serenity in twilight's grasp,
We find the strength, we gently clasp.
An interlude where hearts align,
Aetherial magic, yours and mine.

So let us drift on starlit streams,
In quiet wonders, weave our dreams.
Together in this spectral hue,
Aetherial moments shared by two.

Cosmic Echoes

In the stillness where shadows play,
Cosmic echoes guide our way.
Voices whisper through the dark,
Resonating like a lark.

With stardust scattered on our paths,
We listen close to nature's laughs.
Timeless stories, ages old,
In the night, our hearts are bold.

Stars align to share their grace,
Finding solace in this space.
Every heartbeat, every sigh,
Is a note in the cosmic sky.

Connections felt beyond the veil,
As constellations tell their tale.
Through the galaxies, we reach wide,
In these echoes, love won't hide.

So let us roam where wonders flow,
In cosmic waves, our spirits glow.
Together we will chase the sound,
In echoes of the universe, we are found.

Radiant Networks

In the web of stars we find,
Connections spark, entwined.
Light travels fast, a silent song,
In unity, where we belong.

Through the vast, endless night,
Our dreams take off in flight.
We are threads in cosmic lace,
Weaving time and endless space.

Galaxies dance, colliding grace,
Echoes of a boundless place.
Every heartbeat, every sigh,
A reminder that we fly.

Between the planets, whispers flow,
In every star's gentle glow.
Radiant paths with tales to share,
Every moment sparks a flare.

So let us join this vibrant chase,
Expand our hearts, embrace this space.
Together we rise, ignite the flame,
In this network, we are the same.

The Language of Light

In beams of gold, the sun will speak,
A whisper soft, yet oh so unique.
It travels far, through time and air,
A sacred bond, beyond compare.

Moonbeams dance on tranquil seas,
Softly weaving through the trees.
Each flicker holds a silent phrase,
A symphony in cosmic ways.

Stars will chart their shining tales,
Guiding ships with starlit sails.
In every twinkle, a story told,
A language pure, both brave and bold.

With every dawn, a new decree,
Illuminating what will be.
The colors blend, a painter's dream,
In this light, we find our theme.

Let us listen, hearts aligned,
In the light, our souls unwind.
Together we rise, hearts ignited,
In the glow, our truths united.

Harmonies Among the Planets

In orbits wide, the planets spin,
Each note a truth, where we begin.
Harmony echoes, a cosmic choir,
A dance of worlds that never tire.

Mars sings red, with fiery might,
While Venus glimmers, soft and bright.
Jupiter's roar, a thunderous call,
Saturn's rings, a gentle thrall.

Moons in rhythm, a lunar beat,
In perfect sync, they move discreet.
Uranus flips, a quirky tune,
Neptune's whispers, a misty rune.

Through the void, melodies soar,
Connecting each familiar shore.
Galaxies sway in cosmic grace,
In harmony, we find our place.

So let us join this symphony,
Embrace our roles, eternally.
In every note, life's song we find,
Among the planets, hearts entwined.

Interstellar Kinship

Stars align in cosmic kin,
A bond of light that draws us in.
We share the universe's embrace,
Across the void, we find our place.

In silent realms where shadows play,
Our spirits soar through night and day.
A kinship forged in stellar glow,
In every heartbeat, love will flow.

Through nebulae our dreams take flight,
Guided by the ancient light.
Each echo from the past we hear,
Reminds us we are ever near.

In every galaxy, a story lives,
Of passion, peace, and hope it gives.
Together weaving paths so bright,
In interstellar kinship's light.

So let us reach beyond the stars,
Embrace a life that's truly ours.
Connected by the cosmic thread,
In unity, where dreams are spread.

Celestial Correspondence

In the quiet night, stars align,
Whispers of light, a secret sign.
Dreams woven in cosmic flow,
Hearts united, their glow will show.

Across the span of endless skies,
Messages dance, where hope lies.
Infinite stories in silence heard,
A tapestry bright, in each word.

Galaxies spin, the universe speaks,
In distant lands, love gently seeks.
Through stardust trails, our thoughts ignite,
Connecting souls in the soft twilight.

Together we wander, hand in hand,
Through boundless realms, a timeless land.
Each heartbeat echoes, a radiant song,
In celestial halls where we belong.

The cosmos sings a lullaby sweet,
In every moment, hearts will meet.
Celestial paths, forever entwined,
In the melody of the divine.

Embracing the Universe

Wrapped in starlight, we float and sway,
Every heartbeat a cosmic ballet.
Embracing the vastness, we take flight,
In the dance of day merging with night.

Nebulae cradle our whispered dreams,
Boundless horizons where hope redeems.
We twirl through shadows, in radiant grace,
Finding our truth in this sacred space.

Infinity calls, a soft, warm breath,
In unity found, we conquer death.
Together we rise, fueled by desire,
Igniting the stars, we blaze like fire.

Cosmic wonders wrapped in our gaze,
Love's gentle touch ignites the blaze.
In every connection, the universe sighs,
As we spin through the heavens, kissing the skies.

We bridge the gaps of time and light,
In the embrace of the endless night.
With every breath, our spirits unite,
In love's embrace, pure and bright.

Orbits of Togetherness

In celestial paths, we find our way,
Circling the sun at the break of day.
Gravity binds our hearts so tight,
In the dance of planets, we ignite.

Through rings of Saturn, we glide and spin,
Exploring the cosmos, where love begins.
Each orbit a tale, our souls entwined,
In the vast expanse, our stars aligned.

Comets of joy paint the night sky,
With trails of laughter, they shimmer and fly.
Together we journey through dark and light,
In the embrace of galaxies, holding tight.

A mosaic of life in motion flows,
As the universe weaves its intricate prose.
With each revolving turn, we thrive,
In orbits of togetherness, we come alive.

Eternal companions, we soar and roam,
Finding in starlight, a shared home.
Friends in the cosmos, our spirits blend,
In the beauty of time, love has no end.

The Language of Stars

In the night sky, secrets unfold,
Every star a story, waiting to be told.
Silently they sparkle, in wisdom and grace,
Translating dreams in the cosmic space.

Twinkling lights speak in melodies sweet,
The pulse of the universe, a rhythmic beat.
Each constellation paints a shared lore,
Uniting our hearts to seek evermore.

In the glow of the moon, whispers ignite,
Guiding our paths through the infinite night.
Their glimmers of hope spark the divine,
In the language of stars, our fates align.

With every glance, connections grow strong,
In the map of the heavens, we each belong.
Together we learn, basking in light,
Transcending the boundaries, hearts taking flight.

A cosmic embrace wraps us so tight,
In the tapestry woven, we find our light.
In the language of stars, love always reigns,
Binding our souls in invisible chains.

Dance of the Wandering Stars

In the sky where shadows play,
Stars twinkle, drifting away.
Each one tells a tale of old,
Wonders of the night unfold.

Galaxies spin in cosmic grace,
In their waltz, we find our place.
Whispers of the past ignite,
Guiding us through endless night.

With every step, we chase the light,
Comets blaze, a stunning sight.
Together in this vast expanse,
We share the stars, a timeless dance.

Beneath the moon's soft silver glow,
With dreams that ebb and flow,
We find our hearts in cosmic ties,
As worlds collide and love replies.

Through the void, we journey far,
Bound together, here we are.
In the dance of wandering stars,
Our love shines bright, no matter how far.

Love Across Lightyears

In the silence of the night,
You are my guiding light.
With every pulse, you call to me,
Across the vast infinity.

Two hearts beating out of time,
A love like distant stars that rhyme.
Through the echoes, soft and clear,
I sense your warmth, I feel you near.

With every glance, the cosmos bends,
Our story written, as fate intends.
In the dance of twilight skies,
We bridge the dark with starlit sighs.

Though galaxies may keep us apart,
Our love transcends the deepest dark.
Across the void, our whispers soar,
In this universe, forevermore.

Lightyears cannot dim our flame,
In every star, I see your name.
Together we soar through endless dreams,
A love as boundless as it seems.

Astral Affinity

In the night where shadows blend,
We find a magic that won't end.
Galaxies swirl with every glance,
An astral sparkle, a cosmic dance.

Together, we traverse the skies,
With stardust dreams in our eyes.
In the universe, we carve our way,
In endless night, we choose to play.

Constellations whisper our names,
In their light, our love remains.
Through the twists of fate we flow,
In this bond, we come to know.

With meteors as our guiding force,
We ride the waves of celestial course.
Two souls entwined, forever free,
In the cosmic sea, just you and me.

Every heartbeat, a star ignites,
In the canvas of moonlit nights.
Through the universe, we are drawn,
A love like starlight, forever strong.

Chasing Comets Together

When comets streak through the night,
We chase their trails, a wondrous sight.
Hand in hand, we laugh and play,
In the glow of the Milky Way.

With every flash, a wish we make,
In this universe, our hearts awake.
Across the void, our spirits soar,
In this chase, we yearn for more.

Each comet tells a tale of dreams,
In their tails, our laughter gleams.
We dance beneath the cosmic flow,
In every moment, love will grow.

Together, we will ride the stream,
In this journey, we find our dream.
Through the stars, we'll wander far,
Fate entwined, like every star.

In the night, our souls ignite,
Chasing comets, pure delight.
In the echoes of the skies above,
We find the light of endless love.

Galactic Affection

In cosmic dance, we twirl and sway,
Stars align in night's soft ballet.
Your light beams bright, a guiding force,
Together we chart our endless course.

Through nebulae, our whispers blend,
Celestial paths that never end.
With stardust dreams, our hearts ignite,
We soar beyond the veil of night.

In the silence, echoes hum,
With every pulse, love's rhythm comes.
A universe of shared delight,
In galactic arms, we take flight.

Each comet's tail, a promise made,
In this vast sky, our fears will fade.
Cosmic winds will carry our song,
In the heart of space, we belong.

Together we weave our sacred lore,
A tapestry of love to explore.
Galaxies spin, yet still we hold,
This love, a story forever told.

Echoes from the Ether

Whispers travel on the breeze,
Secrets shared with ancient trees.
In twilight's glow, stories awake,
Echoes of all the paths we take.

Through shadows deep, the mysteries play,
Guiding us softly, come what may.
In celestial pulse, we find our tune,
Beneath the watchful gaze of the moon.

In every heartbeat, listen close,
The ether speaks, let dreams propose.
With every sigh, the cosmos sighs,
As starlit hopes begin to rise.

Threads of fate in silken strands,
We dance together, hand in hands.
Through realms of time, our spirits roam,
In echoes, we find our true home.

With every step upon this ground,
The universe whispers, love profound.
Together we forge each starry night,
Echoes of love in endless flight.

Unified in the Sky

Beneath the moon's soft, silver friend,
Two souls unite where skies blend.
With every glance, the world ignites,
In harmony, we take our flights.

Clouds of dreams drift far and wide,
In gentle winds, our hearts collide.
Through endless fields of cosmic art,
We're unified, never apart.

As sun and stars embrace the dawn,
In this vast sky, love's strength is drawn.
With every twinkle, whispers grow,
In evening's hush, our secrets flow.

Together, we paint the evening shade,
With colors bright, our fears will fade.
In constellations, our story spins,
Unified in love, where all begins.

Through storms and calm, we find our way,
In cosmic dance, we forever sway.
Unified in the vast domain,
Our love will bloom, a bright refrain.

Orbiting Love

In the circle of stars, we glide,
Through the vastness, side by side.
Orbiting dreams in silent flight,
Together we chase the glittering light.

With gravity's pull, our hearts collide,
In a cosmic waltz, we cannot hide.
Eclipsed by joy, we dance and spin,
In this endless loop, we both win.

Around the sun, we find our place,
In the rhythm of time and space.
Trailing stardust, soft and warm,
In orbiting love, we weather the storm.

With every turn, a promise made,
In the galaxy's arms, we won't fade.
Bound by passion, like moons embrace,
Orbiting love our endless grace.

With celestial songs, our spirits soar,
In this dance, forevermore.
In every heartbeat, we feel the tie,
Orbiting love beneath the sky.

Milky Way Murmurs

Whispers of starlight, soft and bright,
Dancing through shadows, embracing the night.
Galaxies twinkle, secrets unfold,
Tales of the cosmos, endlessly told.

Nebulas painted in colors so rare,
Filling our hearts with wonder and care.
Rivers of stardust, flowing divine,
Mapping our dreams, in patterns that shine.

Planets in motion, a celestial race,
Each spin a story, each orbit a grace.
Under the vastness, we find our way,
United in mystery, night after day.

Shooting stars whisper as dreams take flight,
We reach for the heavens, hearts burning bright.
In the calm of the night, we pause and sway,
Listening closely to the Milky Way.

A cosmic ballet, where time does bend,
In the glow of the galaxy, we blend and transcend.
Through the void's embrace, we find our peace,
Murmurs of the Milky Way never cease.

Celestial Kinship

In the quiet of night, stars softly gleam,
Together we wander, a mystical dream.
With every heartbeat, the universe sings,
Connected as one, in all of its things.

Galaxies twirl in a delicate dance,
Reflecting our bond, our infinite chance.
Each twinkle a promise, each glow a tie,
Celestial kinship, 'neath the vast sky.

Constellations whisper, tales of old,
In the fabric of time, our journeys unfold.
As comets pass by, and planets align,
We find in each moment, the stars and the divine.

From dusk till dawn, we embrace the light,
Holding each other through darkness and bright.
The cosmos our cradle, the ether our home,
Bound by the heavens, forever we roam.

In the shimmer above, we glimpse our dreams,
Each flicker a hope, or so it seems.
Under the glow of a celestial hymn,
We cherish each heartbeat, our souls thus akin.

Infinity in Our Eyes

Gazing at starlight, forever we find,
Reflections of mysteries held in our minds.
The universe spins, timeless and vast,
Each moment a treasure, each heartbeat amassed.

In the depths of our souls, galaxies reign,
Infinity glimmers, in joy and in pain.
With every new dawn, we reach for the skies,
Finding forever in each other's eyes.

Eternal horizons, painted in grace,
A canvas of wonders, in endless embrace.
Through valleys of shadows, our spirits ignite,
Searching for magic, igniting the night.

Our laughter a spark, our love a flame,
In the vastness of space, we call out each name.
In moments of silence, our hearts intertwine,
We dance with the cosmos, the stars are our sign.

Through wonders and whispers, together we rise,
Holding forever, in the depths of our eyes.
Each rhythm, each heartbeat, a promise we keep,
In infinity's gaze, our spirits go deep.

Soulmates of the Skies

Hand in hand, we wander the night,
Finding our path in the soft starlight.
With whispers of dreams, the sky's lullaby,
We are the soulmates who reach for the high.

Through constellations, our stories are spun,
In the cosmic embrace, we're two becoming one.
Together we sail on the wings of the breeze,
As galaxies shimmer, we greet with ease.

Beneath the moon's gaze, our hearts lay bare,
Tales of the cosmos, we tenderly share.
Every shooting star, a wish we release,
In the universe's arms, we find our peace.

With laughter like comets, our spirits ignite,
In the vastness above, we dance through the night.
Soulmates of skies, forever we'll soar,
In the silence of space, our hearts will explore.

With each tender moment, our story enchains,
Bound by the whispers of love that remains.
Through the twilight's embrace, we endlessly strive,
In the canvas of stardust, we eternally thrive.

Veils of Starlight

In the still of the night, whispers flow,
Veils of starlight, a celestial show.
Gentle glimmers dance on the lake,
Awakening dreams that softly awake.

Moonbeams brush the earth's gentle cheek,
Painting shadows where silence speaks.
In this magic, our spirits entwine,
Lost in the glow of the divine.

Clouds drift softly, like thoughts on the breeze,
Carrying wishes across the seas.
Each twinkle and flicker tells a tale,
Written in starlight, soft and pale.

Hope is a comet, swift as it flies,
Leaving trails of wonder in darkened skies.
We reach for the heavens, where dreams take flight,
Guided by veils of shimmering light.

With every breath, the cosmos sighs,
A symphony sung by the stars that rise.
In veils of starlight, we find our place,
Bound by the universe's tender embrace.

Ties of the Universe

In the tapestry vast, threads intertwine,
Spirits connect through the fabric of time.
Galaxies spin in a cosmic dance,
Weaving our destinies, fate's sweet chance.

From atoms to stars, a rhythm we share,
Echoes of life in the weightless air.
Each heartbeat resonates with the whole,
Boundless love flowing from soul to soul.

Gravity pulls, like a lover's embrace,
In the universe's arms, we find our place.
Dimensions unfold, mysteries astound,
In the ties of the cosmos, true peace is found.

Waves of existence, like whispers in space,
Remind us of dreams that time can't erase.
In the quiet, we listen, we learn,
For every moment, our hearts gently yearn.

Together we're woven, in light and in dark,
With starlit adventures that spark a new arc.
Through the cosmos we wander, hand in hand,
Eternal connections, forever we stand.

Night Sky Narratives

Beneath the dark veil, stories unfold,
Tales of the brave, of the young and the old.
Constellations whisper ancient lore,
In the night sky, adventures galore.

Each star a chapter, in the sky's grand tale,
Guiding lost dreamers, setting their sail.
The moon paints wisdom with silver light,
Illuminating paths in the heart of the night.

Echoes of laughter, and shadows of tears,
Intertwined moments, spanning the years.
From silent wishes to dreams that ignite,
The night sky holds stories, out of our sight.

A canvas of darkness, splashed with bright dreams,
Crafting realities from starlit beams.
In nocturnal realms, where wishes take flight,
The universe listens, with all of its might.

So gaze to the heavens, breathe in the vast,
Find solace in night, let your heart fly fast.
For every soul has a narrative bright,
Written in stardust, embraced by the night.

Harmonious Horizons

At the edge of the world, where colors collide,
Harmonious horizons, where dreams coincide.
With each dawn, a symphony starts,
Filling the air, touching our hearts.

The golden sun rises, a maestro in sky,
Painting the clouds as it whispers goodbye.
In the twilight glow, shades blend and play,
Crafting a masterpiece, ending the day.

Fields of lavender sway with the breeze,
Their melodies echo, inviting us to seize.
Nature composes a song, sweet and clear,
In harmonious whispers, for all who will hear.

Mountains stand proud, guardians in grace,
Holding the secrets of time and space.
With rivers that flow, forever they'll run,
In the dance of existence, we are all one.

So let us embrace these horizons so wide,
In the beauty of moments, our hearts open wide.
For life is a canvas, and each day we find,
A harmony waiting, both gentle and kind.

A Dance with the Stars

In the velvet night sky, they twirl,
A silver waltz beneath the moon,
Each bright spark whispers a tale,
Of dreams that dare to soar and swoon.

Galaxies spin in a silent embrace,
While comets trail in a fiery flight,
Every heartbeat joins the chase,
A dance with fate, a dance with light.

Planets sway in their cosmic path,
The universe hums a timeless tune,
Stars align, igniting the math,
In this grand ballroom, under the moon.

Echoes of laughter fill the air,
As constellations weave their song,
A tapestry rich, beyond compare,
Where moments stretch and belong.

So let us lose ourselves tonight,
In the spiral of time and space,
For in this dance, we find our light,
A journey shared, a warm embrace.

Celestial Serenade

Awash in the glow of twilight's grace,
The stars ignite a cosmic tune,
Each note drips from the heavens' face,
A melody whispered to the moon.

Planets pulse in harmonic delight,
As cosmic winds carry the sound,
In the darkness, a symphony bright,
Where lost souls are finally bound.

Nebulas glow, a painter's brush,
Colors swirl in a vibrant dance,
In this moment, there's no rush,
Just the universe's tender romance.

As meteors streak like wishes made,
We listen closely to their flight,
In this serenade, dreams cascade,
Igniting hopes in the fading light.

So close your eyes and let it flow,
A celestial song in your heart,
For in the silence, we truly know,
The universe plays its vital part.

Ties Beyond Time

In the fabric of night, threads intertwine,
Connections forged in unseen threads,
Hearts beat softly, in rhythm, align,
A timeless dance where the journey spreads.

Through echoes of ages, whispers descend,
A bond unbroken by space or fate,
With every heartbeat, we transcend,
Embracing love past the hands of late.

Stars remind us of paths we've traced,
As galaxies pull with gentle sighs,
In the cosmic quilt, our dreams interlaced,
Binding together, where infinity lies.

These ties extend through the dark unknown,
In the quiet, we find our way,
With every pulse, we're not alone,
Connected forever, come what may.

So let us dance in this boundless space,
Two souls entwined in rhythm's flow,
For in this moment, we find our place,
In timeless love, we come to know.

Cosmic Heartstrings

With every heartbeat, the cosmos sings,
A symphony born from stardust dreams,
Life's tapestry woven with cosmic strings,
Pulled gently along, or so it seems.

Through the darkness, light begins to weave,
These heartstrings echo through space and time,
In the depths of night, we learn to believe,
That love's melody is always sublime.

In the vast expanse, our souls entwined,
Dancing like comets, bright and bold,
A fusion of destinies, boldly defined,
Where stories unfold, and secrets are told.

Each star a note in our galactic score,
Pulsing softly with every embrace,
Together we journey to seek and explore,
In the rhythm of life, we find our place.

So let the universe play on its strings,
As we sway to the beat of what's true,
In the cosmic dance, our spirit takes wings,
Forever in tune, just me and you.